THE
55 BEST BROWNIES
IN THE WORLD

ALSO BY HONEY AND LARRY ZISMAN

The 47 Best Chocolate Chip Cookies in the World
Super Sweets
The Great American Peanut Butter Book
The Great International Dessert Cookbook
The Burger Book
Chocolate Fantasies

THE
55 BEST BROWNIES
IN THE WORLD

★★★★★★★★★★★★★★★★★★★★★★★★★★

*The Recipes That Won the Great
American Brownie Bake Contest*

HONEY AND LARRY
ZISMAN

St. Martin's Press ★ New York

Library of Congress Cataloging-in-Publication Data

Zisman, Honey.
    The 55 best brownies in the world : the recipes that won the
nationwide great American brownie bake / Honey and Larry Zisman.
        p.   cm.
    Includes index.
    ISBN 0-312-05862-4
    1. Brownies (Cookery)   I. Zisman, Larry.   II. Title.   III. Title:
The 55 best brownies in the world.
TX771.Z57   1991
641.8'653—dc20   90-27849
                                                                                                             CIP

First Edition: August 1991

10 9 8 7 6 5 4 3 2 1

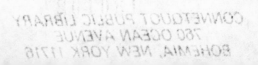

You'll never wear a frownie
when you make yourself a brownie.

THE
55 BEST BROWNIES
IN THE WORLD

BROWNIES IN OUR HEARTS, MINDS . . . AND MOUTHS

★★★★★★★★★★★★★★★★★★★★★★★★★★★★★

Can anyone honestly question the widespread wisdom that brownies top the list of quintessential, favorite, down-home, comfort foods?

Indeed, it is estimated that more than 2 billion of these rich little squares—or bars, depending on how you cut them—are consumed every twelve months.

Assuming a modest average size of 2 inches by 2 inches by 1 inch high (and most of them are not so modest, but bigger and better since bigger *is* better when it comes to brownies), 2 billion brownies would cover a football field (including both end zones) to a depth of 80 feet. Try returning a kick-off while running in soft, moist chocolate cake studded with nuts and rising way over your head.

Looking at these 2 billion brownies another way, a stack would form a tower over 31,000 miles high. That would be 5,700 times as high as Mt. Everest, the highest mountain on Earth, or 115,000 times as high as the Sears Tower in Chicago, the tallest building in the world.

Finally, if you placed all those brownies side by side they would wrap around the world two-and-a-half times.

That's a lot of brownies.

And brownies are not just some new taste treat that is fashionable for just a day or two.

The Sears, Roebuck catalog for Spring, 1896, contained a long list of groceries that you could order by mail. In addition to maple caramels, chicken gumbo soup, walnut catsup, essence of anchovies, and everything else, there they were, listed under "Fancy Crackers, Biscuits, Etc.": "Brownies in 1-lb. papers."

The cost? Just $1.50 per dozen, or 14 cents each.

Not only are brownies longtime favorites and delicious to eat, but scientific proof exists that brownies have a higher purpose beyond pure enjoyment and decadence: absolution.

Langer Associates, a market research company in New York City, conducted interviews for *Self* magazine exploring women's career choices and the conflicts these women feel when deciding how to allocate time and commitments between their careers and their children.

Researchers noted that women surveyed said repeatedly that they baked brownies to assuage the guilt they felt for not having enough time to spend with their children.

Besides being the right food for the psyche, brownies are also the right color.

In a special Executive Fashion section, *Business Week* magazine noted that brown, once shunned, is now gaining acceptability as a color for men's business suits. Unfortunately, the right shade of brown for a suit is not chocolate but more of a taupe—a bluish-brown. But corporate America is coming around.

And *People* magazine, the ultimate arbiter of what's hot and what's not, has declared that black, the "in" color of the 1980s, has been replaced in the 1990s by none other than brown.

4

For these reasons and more, there can be no doubt that brownies are the ultimate treat!

And collected right here are the ultimate of these ultimate treats, the 55 winning recipes in The Great American Brownie Bake. This contest attracted thousands of entries from coast to coast . . . and from out west in Hawaii and up north in Alaska and Canada.

So look through these pages, pick out your favorites, and bake the best brownies in the land. We love them all and every one is a winner.

COMFORT, JOY, AND SATISFACTION AWAIT YOU!

OH, THE AGONY . . .
OH, THE ECSTASY!
★★★★★★★★★★★★★★★★★★★★★★★★★★★★★

Conducting a national brownie contest can take a lot of effort and energy . . . Oh, the agony!

On the other hand, conducting a national brownie contest can also be a lot of fun and a lot of very, very good tasting . . . Oh, the ecstasy!

One minor agony was the work involved in preparing and sending out hundreds and hundreds of contest announcements to newspapers and magazines throughout the United States and Canada.

Another minor agony was opening close to 3,500 envelopes containing all kinds of brownie recipes and carefully recording and filing all these entries.

But, most definitely and most happily, the *ecstasy* was much, much greater than the *agony*.

Reading through all the recipes and seeing the imagination, creativity, and interesting variations on such a basic, traditional treat was a job, yes, but a very pleasant one.

And then there was the even greater enjoyment in preparing and tasting brownies, brownies, and more brownies. It was the proverbial dirty job that someone had to do and . . . thank goodness . . . we were the ones who had to do it.

It wasn't quick work, since so many brownies had to be savored and judged.

It wasn't easy work choosing the winners, since there were so many delicious entries.

And it wasn't the type of work that you quit at five o'clock and put out of your mind, since you thought about all those great brownies until you fell asleep late at night.

But it was very worthwhile work finding the 55 best brownies in the world, the source of greatest enjoyment for brownie lovers everywhere.

What agony?

Now there is only ecstasy for everyone!

HOW TO TELL WHEN YOUR BROWNIES ARE DONE BAKING

★★★★★★★★★★★★★★★★★★★★★★★★★★★★

One of the many nice things about brownies is that they can be enjoyed in different ways—very moist, a little moist, a little crisp, very crisp, and anything in between—depending on your own personal tastes.

Obviously, the less time you bake your brownies the moister they will be, while the longer you bake them the crisper they will be.

If you like your brownies on the moist side, when a recipe gives a range of cooking times, such as "bake for 20 to 25 minutes," check them at the 18- to 20-minute mark. Stick a toothpick in the brownies and, if some brownie sticks to the toothpick, you have a moister brownie. Another test is to press the top of the brownies. If the indentation of your finger remains, the brownie will be moister than if the indentation springs back. Still another test is to observe the sides of the pan: the brownies will be moister if they have not pulled away from the sides.

However, if you want crisper brownies, keep testing with a toothpick until it comes out clean, keep pushing the top of the brownies until it bounces back, or continue baking until the brownies pull away from the sides of the pan.

Several other hints you should know:

- Brownies made with dates, raisins, and other fruits or juices tend to be extra-moist and usually require longer baking times.

- Different ovens have different actual baking temperatures inside, even if set to the same temperature on the dial. Remember to adjust the baking time depending on how "fast" or "slow" your oven is.
- The size of the baking pan also affects baking time. If the recipe calls for a 9-inch square pan and all you have is an 8-inch square pan, the baking time will be longer. Conversely, if you use a larger pan than the recipe calls for, the baking time will be shorter.

BROWNIE CAMERAS—*Easy-to-use cameras introduced by Kodak in 1900, and particularly suited for taking pictures of people eating brownies.*

MOLASSES MINT BROWNIES

RUTH M. STEUR, CORAL SPRINGS, FLORIDA

½ cup margarine, melted and cooled
¼ cup molasses
1 cup sugar
2 eggs
¾ cup sifted flour
¼ teaspoon salt
16 chocolate mint wafers, broken into pieces
½ teaspoon vanilla
½ cup chopped walnuts

Preheat oven to 350°F.

Mix together margarine, molasses, and sugar. Add eggs, one at a time, beating after each addition. Set aside.

Sift flour and salt and add to molasses mixture. Mix in wafers and vanilla.

Pour one half of the batter into a greased 8-inch square pan. Sprinkle walnuts over top. Evenly cover with remaining batter.

Bake for 35 to 40 minutes. Let cool, remove from pan, and cut into 2-inch squares. *Yield: 16 brownies*

MISSISSIPPI MUD BARS

★★★★★★★★★★★★★★★★★★★★★★★★★★★

REBECCA STEVENSON, FAIRFAX, VIRGINIA

1 cup unsalted butter, at room temperature
2 cups sugar
4 eggs, at room temperature
1 teaspoon vanilla
1½ cups flour
3 tablespoons cocoa powder
1½ cups flaked coconut
1 jar (7 ounces) marshmallow creme
Mud Frosting (recipe follows)

Preheat oven to 350°F.

Cream butter and sugar until fluffy. Beat in eggs, one at a time, and blend in vanilla. Set aside.

Combine flour and cocoa powder and then beat into butter mixture. Fold in coconut and pecans.

Spoon batter into a greased 9 × 13-inch pan, spreading evenly.

Bake for 35 to 40 minutes or until toothpick tests clean in center. Remove from oven and immediately spoon marshmallow creme

over brownies. As marshmallow creme melts, spread gently.
Let brownies cool completely and top with Mud Frosting.
Cut into 2 × 3-inch bars.   *Yield: 18 brownies*

MUD FROSTING

*½ cup unsalted butter, at room
   temperature
1 teaspoon vanilla
4 cups confectioners' sugar
⅓ cup cocoa powder
½ cup evaporated milk*

Cream butter and vanilla. Set aside.
Combine sugar and cocoa powder and gradually beat into butter
mixture, alternating with milk. Continue beating until frosting is light
and fluffy, about 3 to 5 minutes.

---

*The legal name of Harry Longbaugh (1870–1909) was Henry
Brown. He was better known, however, as that famous westerner the
Sundance Kid.*

KAHLUA BROWNIES

★★★★★★★★★★★★★★★★★★★★★★★★★★★

JANET J. SMITH, PRICEVILLE, ONTARIO, canada

> 1¼ cups flour
> ¼ teaspoon baking powder
> ½ teaspoon salt
> ½ cup butter or margarine
> ¾ cup brown sugar
> 1 large egg
> ¼ cup plus 1 tablespoon Kahlua or any
>   coffee liqueur
> 1 cup (6 ounces) semi-sweet chocolate chips
> ¼ cup chopped walnuts
> Brown Butter Icing (recipe follows)

Preheat oven to 350°F.

Sift together flour, baking powder, and salt. Set aside.

Cream butter, sugar, and egg. Stir in ¼ cup coffee liqueur and flour mixture, blending well. Fold in chocolate chips and walnuts.

Spread mixture into a 9-inch square pan and bake for 30 minutes.

Remove from oven and let cool slightly. Brush top with remaining tablespoon of coffee liqueur.

After brownies are completely cooled, spread with Brown Butter Icing. Cut into 2×2-inch squares.

Yield: 16 brownies

BROWN BUTTER ICING

2 tablespoons butter
1 tablespoon coffee liqueur
2 teaspoons cream
1¼ cups sifted confectioners' sugar

Heat butter until lightly browned. Remove from heat and add coffee liqueur, cream, and sugar. Beat until smooth.

Lester Raymond Brown and his band, billed under the name "Les Brown and His Band of Renown," were popular with audiences throughout the United States and Europe during the 1940s, 1950s, and 1960s. They built their reputation as a good swing band playing in the pop field . . . and one of their vocalists in the 1940s was Doris Day.

DODGE DARTS

★★★★★★★★★★★★★★★★★★★★★★★★★

PAMELA LAMBING, KILL DEVIL HILLS, NORTH CAROLINA

4 ounces unsweetened chocolate
¾ cup butter
2 cups sugar
4 eggs, beaten
1 cup flour
½ teaspoon salt
1 teaspoon vanilla
1 cup nuts
Chocolate Frosting (recipe follows)

Preheat oven to 350°F.

Melt chocolate in a saucepan or a double boiler over hot water. Set aside.

Cream butter and sugar in a large mixing bowl. Stir in melted chocolate. Add eggs, flour, salt, vanilla, and nuts, mixing well.

Spread batter in a greased 9 × 13-inch pan and bake for 25 to 30 minutes.

Remove from oven and let cool. Spread Chocolate Frosting over top and cut into 2 × 2½-inch bars.   *Yield: 20 brownies*

CHOCOLATE FROSTING

½ ounce unsweetened chocolate
1 tablespoon butter
2 tablespoons milk
¾ cup confectioners' sugar

Place chocolate, butter, and milk in a saucepan or double boiler and heat over simmering water, stirring constantly, until chocolate and butter have melted. Remove from heat.

Slowly add sugar and beat until mixture is spreadable.

Brownstone is a soft, reddish sandstone that was used during the 1800s in the construction of many houses in northeastern American cities. In New York City, the wealthy people who lived in these houses got to be known as "brownstones," and now these very desirable rowhouses themselves are called brownstones.

What better place to serve brownies than in a brownstone?

MACADAMIA MOCHA BROWNIES

★★★★★★★★★★★★★★★★★★★★★★★★★★★★

DON FERGUSON, U.S. NAVY (RET), HONOLULU, HAWAII

> 2 cups finely ground graham-cracker
>   crumbs
> 1 cup chopped, unsalted macadamia nuts
> 3 heaping teaspoons instant coffee powder
> 1 teaspoon vanilla
> 1⅓ cups sweetened condensed milk
> ¼ teaspoon salt
> 1 cup (6 ounces) semi-sweet chocolate
>   chips
> Confectioners' sugar (optional)

Preheat oven to 350°F.

Mix together graham-cracker crumbs, nuts, coffee powder, vanilla, milk, salt, and chocolate chips, stirring until well blended.

Pour batter into a greased 8-inch square pan.

Bake for 25 to 30 minutes. Remove from oven, let cool slightly, and, while still warm, cut into 2-inch squares.

If desired, dust with confectioners' sugar.

Yield: 16 brownies

BANANA-FANA BROWNIES

★★★★★★★★★★★★★★★★★★★★★★★★★★★★

TAMBRA BIRKEBAK, SEATTLE, WASHINGTON

2 ounces unsweetened chocolate
⅓ cup butter or margarine
1 cup sugar
2 eggs
2 tablespoons peanut butter
½ cup mashed ripe banana
1 cup flour
¼ teaspoon salt
½ teaspoon baking powder
¼ teaspoon baking soda

Preheat oven to 350°F.

Melt chocolate and butter together in a saucepan or a double boiler over simmering water. Stir in sugar, eggs, peanut butter, and banana.

Remove from heat and add flour, salt, baking powder, and baking soda. Mix well.

Bake for 25 to 30 minutes in a greased 8-inch square pan. Remove from oven, let cool, and then cut into 2-inch squares.

Yield: 16 brownies

CARAMELASTIC FANTASTIC BROWNIES

★★★★★★★★★★★★★★★★★★★★★★★★★★★★

LINDA J. DIETZLER, RICHFIELD, MINNESOTA

14 ounces caramels
1 can (14 ounces) sweetened condensed
  milk
1 cup plus 1 tablespoon shortening
2 cups sugar
4 eggs
¾ cup cocoa powder
¼ cup milk
1½ cups flour
1 teaspoon salt
1 teaspoon baking powder
1 cup (6 ounces) semi-sweet chocolate
  chips
1 cup chopped nuts

Preheat oven to 350°F.
Place caramels and sweetened condensed milk in a heavy saucepan

and cook over low heat, stirring often, until caramels are completely melted and ingredients are blended.

While caramels are cooking, place shortening in a heavy saucepan and cook over low heat until melted. Remove from heat and set aside to cool.

Beat sugar and eggs and then add cocoa powder, milk, and cooled shortening. Set aside.

Sift flour, salt, and baking powder and add to chocolate mixture, beating thoroughly. Stir in chocolate chips and ½ cup of the nuts.

Place two-thirds of the batter in a greased 9 × 13-inch pan and bake for 12 minutes.

Remove brownies from oven and pour melted caramels over top. Sprinkle remaining ½ cup of nuts over the caramels.

Drop remaining third of the batter by teaspoonfuls evenly over brownies and smooth out top using dampened hands or a knife. (Be careful not to burn your hands on the sides of the hot pan.) Using a knife, cut through brownie batter to marbleize.

Return pan to oven and bake for an additional 25 to 28 minutes. Remove from oven and cover with aluminum foil for 1 hour.

Refrigerate with foil still on for another hour or until cooled.

Cut into 1½ × 3-inch bars.

Yield: 24 brownies

EASY PEANUT BUTTER DELIGHTS

★★★★★★★★★★★★★★★★★★★★★★★★★★

REGINA J. ALBRIGHT, LAS VEGAS, NEVADA

½ cup margarine
¾ cup evaporated milk
2 cups sugar
¾ cup peanut butter
3 cups quick oats
½ cup coconut
1 teaspoon vanilla
1 cup mini-marshmallows
2 cups (12 ounces) chocolate chips

Place margarine, milk, and sugar in a saucepan and heat to a boil, stirring occasionally. Remove from heat and set aside.

Mix together peanut butter, oats, coconut, vanilla, marshmallows, and chocolate chips. Add sugar mixture and stir well.

Press mixture into a greased 9 × 13-inch pan and let cool.

Cut into 2-inch squares.

Yield: 24 brownies

NO-BAKE FUDGE BROWNIES

★★★★★★★★★★★★★★★★★★★★★★★★★★★★★

DARLENE PRICE-NEWCITY, SAVANNAH, GEORGIA

12 ounces semi-sweet chocolate
1 can (14 ounces) sweetened condensed
milk
2½ cups (9 ounces) finely crushed
chocolate wafers
1 cup chopped nuts

Melt chocolate over hot—not boiling—water, stirring until smooth. Remove from heat and add milk, chocolate wafers, and ½ cup of the nuts. Stir until well blended.

Spread with dampened hands into a greased 8-inch square pan. Press remaining ½ cup of nuts into top of brownies.

Let cool completely and then cut into 2-inch squares.

Yield: 16 brownies

KENTUCKY BLACK WALNUT DELIGHTS

★★★★★★★★★★★★★★★★★★★★★★★★★★

MRS. GAIL MASTERS ROE, WILMORE, KENTUCKY

1 cup finely chopped peeled apples
Apple peels
1⅓ cups water
1 cup quick cooking oats
½ cup butter or margarine, softened
1 cup packed light brown sugar
1 cup sugar
2 eggs
1½ cups flour
½ cup cocoa powder
1 teaspoon baking powder
1 teaspoon baking soda
¼ teaspoon cinnamon
1 cup chopped Kentucky black walnuts
    (English walnuts or hickory nuts may be
    substituted)
Whipped cream or confectioners' sugar

Preheat oven to 350°F.

Set aside chopped peeled apples.

Heat apple peels and water to boiling. Remove and discard peels. Add oats to water, stir, and then set aside for about 15 minutes.

Cream butter, sugars, and eggs until light and fluffy. Add oat-and-water mixture and blend well. Set aside.

Combine flour, cocoa, baking powder, baking soda, and cinnamon and add to oat mixture. Mix well. Stir in chopped apples and walnuts.

Pour batter into a greased and floured 9 × 13-inch pan. Bake for 30 to 35 minutes or until wooden toothpick inserted in center comes out clean.

Let cool, top with whipped cream or confectioners' sugar, and cut into 2-inch squares.

Yield: 24 brownies

In English and Scottish folklore, brownies are tiny elves who do helpful tasks around the house during the night. However, brownies can develop a mischievous streak, and they will leave when criticized or rewarded with anything other than cream, milk, or bread. Perhaps brownies would have a more tolerant attitude if they were given brownies instead of just bread.

TRIPPPLE CHOCOLATE BROWNIES

★★★★★★★★★★★★★★★★★★★★★★★★★★★★

SUZANNE COLASANTO, NEW HAVEN, CONNECTICUT

¾ cup flour
¼ teaspoon baking soda
¼ teaspoon salt
⅓ cup butter
¾ cup sugar
2 tablespoons water
6 ounces semi-sweet chocolate
1 teaspoon vanilla
2 eggs
½ cup (3 ounces) white-chocolate chips
½ cup (3 ounces) milk-chocolate chips
½ cup finely chopped nuts

Preheat oven to 325°F.

Combine flour, baking soda, and salt. Set aside.

In a saucepan combine butter, sugar, and water and heat just to a boil. Remove from heat and add semi-sweet chocolate and vanilla. Stir until chocolate has melted and mixture is smooth. Add eggs, one at a time, beating well after each addition. Gradually blend in flour mixture. Stir in white-chocolate chips, milk-chocolate chips, and nuts.

Spread batter in a greased 8-inch square pan and bake for 30 to 35 minutes.

Cut into 2-inch squares.

Yield: 16 brownies

REMARKABLE RHUBARB BITES

★★★★★★★★★★★★★★★★★★★★★★★★★★★

BEVERLY J. SHIELDS, PORT CRANE, NEW YORK

2 cups diced rhubarb
1 cup sugar
½ cup shortening
1 cup brown sugar
1 egg
1 teaspoon baking soda
¼ teaspoon salt
1 teaspoon cinnamon
2 cups flour
½ teaspoon vanilla
Confectioners' sugar

Preheat oven to 350°F.

Mix together rhubarb and ½ cup of the sugar. Set aside.

Cream shortening, remaining ½ cup of sugar, and brown sugar. Add egg and then stir in baking soda, salt, cinnamon, and flour. Stir in vanilla, then rhubarb mixture.

Place batter in a greased and floured 9 × 13-inch pan and bake for 40 to 45 minutes.

Let cool, sprinkle with confectioners' sugar, and cut into 2-inch squares.

Yield: 24 brownies

No visit to Denver is complete without a stay at the legendary Brown Palace Hotel, downtown on Seventeenth Street. The hotel was built in 1892, and not only is it extravagantly decorated, but it offers guests extraordinary service, elegant dining in the Palace Arms restaurant, and afternoon tea with harp music in the lobby atrium.

There are many features of architectural, artistic, and historic interest in the Brown Palace. These include tiers of cast-iron balconies overlooking the nine-story lobby, with its stained-glass ceiling; extensive use of onyx; historic murals, wallpaper containing 14-carat gold leaf; hand-carved wooden French military band figures; a Chinese Chippendale silver centerpiece; eighteenth-century wine coolers; and papier-mâché golden eagles that are the actual parade decorations used during Napoleon's march from the Arc de Triomphe to Notre Dame when he was crowned Emperor.

The Brown Palace Hotel got its name from the man who built it, Henry C. Brown.

PECAN RIBBON BROWNIES

★★★★★★★★★★★★★★★★★★★★★★★★★★★

JEAN FURNISS, ORIENT, OHIO

½ cup sugar
⅓ cup shortening
3 tablespoons water
6 ounces milk or semi-sweet chocolate
1 teaspoon vanilla
2 eggs
¾ cup flour
¼ teaspoon baking soda
½ teaspoon salt
Pecan Filling (recipe follows)

Preheat oven to 350°F.

Put sugar, shortening, and water in a heavy saucepan and heat to boiling, stirring constantly. Remove from heat and add chocolate and vanilla. Beat in eggs, one at a time. Set aside.

Sift flour, baking soda, and salt and gradually stir into chocolate mixture.

Using slightly dampened hands, spread three-quarters of the batter into a greased 8-inch square pan. Spread with Pecan Filling and top with remaining quarter of the brownie batter.

Bake for 25 to 30 minutes. Remove from oven and let cool. Cut into 2-inch squares.

Yield: 16 brownies

PECAN FILLING

1 egg white
1 tablespoon water
1 teaspoon vanilla
½ cup sugar
2 cups finely chopped pecans
1 tablespoon flour
¾ teaspoon salt

Beat egg white until foamy. Add water and vanilla and gradually beat in sugar. Set aside.

Mix together pecans, flour, and salt and fold into egg mixture.

BROWN BUCKS—*Late 1800s lunch-counter slang for buckwheat cakes.*

LUAU BROWNIES

★★★★★★★★★★★★★★★★★★★★★★★★★★★

ALICE E. SIMPSON, TRUMBULL, CONNECTICUT

2 ounces unsweetened chocolate
¾ cup shortening or margarine
1½ cups sugar
1 teaspoon vanilla
3 eggs
1 cup flour
1 teaspoon baking powder
⅓ cup macadamia nuts, chopped
1 can (8¼ ounces) crushed pineapple,
  drained

Preheat oven to 350°F.

Melt chocolate in a saucepan or a double boiler over simmering water. Set aside to cool.

Combine shortening, sugar, and vanilla and beat until fluffy. Add eggs and beat well. Set aside.

Sift together flour and baking powder and add to egg mixture. Beat until just combined.

Divide batter in half.

Add melted chocolate and nuts to one half of the batter and add pineapple to other half.

Place alternate spoonfuls of each batter in a greased 9 × 13-inch pan. Bake for 20 to 25 minutes.

Remove from oven and let cool. Cut into squares about 2 × 2 inches.

Yield: 24 brownies

The Cleveland Browns, a National Football League team, first took the field in 1946. Their name, the winning entry in a contest, was inspired by "Brown Bomber" Joe Louis, who was the heavyweight champion of the world from 1937 to 1949 and very popular at that time.

By coincidence, the Cleveland Browns' first coach was Paul Brown, who gained considerable fame coaching both college and professional football.

TARTE AU CHOCOLAT

★★★★★★★★★★★★★★★★★★★★★★★★★★★

DIANNE FOLEY HEAREY, SHAKER HEIGHTS, OHIO

PASTRY SHELL

1 cup flour
¼ cup packed light brown sugar
1 ounce unsweetened chocolate, grated
½ cup butter, well chilled and cut into
   pieces
2 tablespoons milk
1 teaspoon vanilla

Put flour, sugar, and chocolate in food processor or large mixing bowl. Add butter pieces and pulse processor or, if using mixer, cut in until mixture is the texture of coarse meal. Mix in milk and vanilla until just blended.

Pastry will be soft and slightly sticky.

Using floured fingertips, pat into bottom and sides of an 8 × 11-inch rectangular or an 11-inch round tart pan with a removable bottom. Set aside.

BROWNIE FILLING

3 ounces semi-sweet chocolate
3 ounces unsweetened chocolate
½ cup butter, at room temperature
1 cup sugar
3 eggs, lightly beaten
2 teaspoons vanilla
½ cup chopped pecans
½ cup (3 ounces) white-chocolate chips
¾ cup flour

Preheat oven to 350°F.

Melt semi-sweet chocolate and unsweetened chocolate in a saucepan or a double boiler over simmering water. Remove from heat and stir in butter. Set aside and let cool to room temperature.

Put chocolate mixture into a large mixing bowl and blend in sugar. Add beaten eggs, one-third at a time, mixing well after each addition. Add vanilla and then stir in nuts and white chocolate. Add flour and mix in with wooden spoon. (Do not use processor or overwork with a mixer.)

Fill Pastry Shell with brownie batter and bake for 20 to 25 minutes or until tester comes out clean in center.

Cool in pan on rack.

CHOCOLATE GLAZE

4 ounces semi-sweet chocolate
¼ cup butter
2 teaspoons vegetable oil

Place chocolate, butter, and oil in a saucepan or a double boiler and heat over simming water, stirring until mixture has melted and is smooth.

Remove from heat and let cool. As mixture cools, it will thicken to a spreadable consistency. Spread glaze over top of baked tart.

Let stand until Chocolate Glaze sets. Remove outer ring of tart pan.

Cut into 2-inch squares or 16 wedges, depending on shape of tart pan used.

Yield: 16 to 20 brownies

BROWNSTONE STATE—*Old nickname for Connecticut, so called because of the brownstone quarries in Portland, in the central part of the state.*

VANILLA CHIPPERS

★★★★★★★★★★★★★★★★★★★★★★★★★★

MRS. HARVEY WILE, WEST HEMPSTEAD, NEW YORK

2 eggs
1 cup sugar
½ cup butter, melted
1 teaspoon vanilla
⅔ cup flour
6 tablespoons cocoa powder
½ teaspoon baking powder
¼ teaspoon salt
1⅔ cups (10 ounces) white-chocolate chips

Preheat oven to 350°F.

Beat eggs well and gradually beat in sugar. Blend in butter and vanilla. Set aside.

Combine flour, cocoa powder, baking powder, and salt and add to egg mixture. Blend together thoroughly. Stir in chips.

Spread batter in a greased 8-inch square pan. Batter will be stiff.

Bake for 25 to 30 minutes until brownies just start to pull away from sides of pan. Let cool completely in pan and then cut into 2-inch squares.   *Yield: 16 brownies*

CHERRY BROWNIES

★★★★★★★★★★★★★★★★★★★★★★★★★★★

HILDA FRANZ, BILOXI, MISSISSIPPI

¼ cup butter or margarine
2 ounces unsweetened chocolate
1 cup sugar
½ teaspoon baking powder
2 eggs
½ cup flour
½ cup chopped nuts
1 teaspoon vanilla
⅓ cup finely chopped maraschino cherries
Chocolate Cherry Frosting (recipe follows)

Preheat oven to 350°F.

Put butter and chocolate in a saucepan or double boiler and melt over simmering water. Remove from heat and blend in sugar and baking powder. Add eggs, one at a time, beating well after each addition. Stir in flour, nuts, vanilla, and maraschino cherries.

Put batter in a greased 8-inch square pan and bake for 30 to 35 minutes. Let cool slightly. Spread with Chocolate Cherry Frosting.

Cut into 2-inch squares.

Yield: 16 brownies

CHOCOLATE CHERRY FROSTING

1 tablespoon butter or margarine
1 ounce unsweetened chocolate
1 cup sifted confectioners' sugar
1 teaspoon vanilla
1 to 2 tablespoons maraschino cherry juice
2 tablespoons finely chopped maraschino
   cherries

Put butter and chocolate in a saucepan or double boiler and melt over simmering water. Remove from heat and mix in sugar and vanilla. Add maraschino cherry juice and stir to a spreading consistency. Add cherries.

Hablot Knight Browne was an English caricaturist who, using the pseudonym "Phiz," was also the original illustrator of many of Charles Dickens's books, including Nicholas Nickleby, David Copperfield, *and* A Tale of Two Cities.

RASPBERRY TRUFFLE BROWNIES

★★★★★★★★★★★★★★★★★★★★★★★★★★★★

SUSAN P. COHEN, PITTSBURGH, PENNSYLVANIA

¾ cup flour
1 teaspoon baking powder
7½ ounces semi-sweet chocolate
½ cup butter
¾ cup brown sugar
2 eggs
1 teaspoon instant coffee powder dissolved
   in 2 tablespoons hot water
Raspberry Truffle Topping (recipe follows)
Chocolate Glaze (recipe follows)

Preheat oven to 325°F.

Combine flour and baking powder. Set aside.

Melt chocolate with butter in a saucepan or a double boiler over simmering water. Set aside to cool slightly.

Beat sugar and eggs. Add chocolate mixture and dissolved coffee. Stir in flour mixture, blending well.

Spread batter in a greased 9-inch square pan and bake for 30 to 35 minutes.

Remove pan from oven and let cool.

Spread Raspberry Truffle Topping over brownies and then drizzle with Chocolate Glaze.

Chill in refrigerator for at least 2 hours. Cut into 2-inch squares.

Yield: 24 brownies

RASPBERRY TRUFFLE TOPPING

3 ounces semi-sweet chocolate
4 ounces cream cheese, softened
2 tablespoons confectioners' sugar
3 tablespoons seedless raspberry preserves

Melt chocolate in a saucepan or double boiler over simmering water. Remove from heat and set aside to cool slightly.

Beat cream cheese until fluffy. Add sugar and preserves and beat in melted chocolate, blending well.

The quick BROWN fox jumped over the lazy yellow dog (so he could get to the brownies on the other side).

CHOCOLATE GLAZE

1½ ounces semi-sweet chocolate
1 teaspoon shortening

Melt chocolate and shortening in a saucepan or double boiler over simmering water. Stir until completely mixed.

"Three-Fingered Brown" was the nickname of Mordecai Peter Centennial Brown, a pitcher with the first outstanding team of modern baseball, the Chicago Cubs of 1906–1910. He had lost half of the index finger on his right hand in a corn shredder when he was a boy, but the accident was a boon to his pitching. The shortened finger allowed him to put a super spin on the ball—giving the pitch one of the wildest curves in baseball history.

Mordecai Brown was the first pitcher to hurl four consecutive shutouts, and in six straight seasons (1906 to 1911) he won twenty or more games, including the twenty-nine won and nine lost in 1908.

DARK CHOCOLATE SWEETIES

★★★★★★★★★★★★★★★★★★★★★★★★★★★

NELLIE LITTLETON, WEST MONROE, LOUISIANA

4 ounces sweet dark chocolate
½ cup butter
2 eggs
1 cup flour
1 cup sugar
Dash salt
1 tablespoon vanilla
½ cup chopped pecans

Preheat oven to 325°F.

Melt chocolate and butter in a saucepan or double boiler over simmering water. Set aside to cool.

Beat eggs for 5 minutes. Add flour, sugar, and salt, mixing well. Blend in chocolate mixture and vanilla. Add pecans.

Put batter into a greased 8-inch pan and bake for 20 to 25 minutes. Cool and cut into 2-inch squares.

Yield: 16 brownies

PEANUT BUTTER DOUBLE DECKERS

★★★★★★★★★★★★★★★★★★★★★★★★★★★★

MARJORIE YORK, MIAMI BEACH, FLORIDA

CHOCOLATE SOUR CREAM LAYER

1 egg
1 cup sugar
½ cup sour cream
⅔ cup flour
⅓ cup cocoa powder
½ teaspoon baking powder
¼ teaspoon baking soda
Dash salt
½ teaspoon vanilla
½ cup chopped walnuts

Preheat oven to 350°F.

Beat together egg and sugar. Add sour cream and beat again. Set aside.

Mix flour, cocoa powder, baking powder, baking soda, and salt. Stir into sour cream mixture. Add vanilla and nuts, mixing well.

Spread batter into a greased 9-inch square pan and then set aside.

PEANUT BUTTER LAYER

½ cup peanut butter
¼ cup butter or margarine
¾ cup sugar
2 eggs
6 tablespoons flour
½ cup (3 ounces) semi-sweet chocolate
  chips

Cream together peanut butter, butter, and sugar. Beat in eggs. Thoroughly mix in flour. Add chocolate chips.

Spoon carefully over Chocolate Sour Cream Layer in pan, spreading evenly.

Bake for 35 to 40 minutes. Remove from oven and let cool. Cut into 2-inch squares.

Yield: 16 brownies

ORANGE MOCHA BROWNIES

★★★★★★★★★★★★★★★★★★★★★★★★★★★

GLORIA T. BOVE, BETHLEHEM, PENNSYLVANIA

¾ cup unsifted flour
¼ teaspoon baking soda
⅓ cup butter
1 cup sugar
2 teaspoons instant coffee powder
2 tablespoons orange juice
1 tablespoon grated orange rind
2 teaspoons orange liqueur
6 ounces semi-sweet chocolate
2 eggs
½ cup chopped nuts

Preheat oven to 325°F.

Combine flour and baking soda. Set aside.

In a medium saucepan, combine butter, sugar, coffee powder, orange juice, orange rind, and liqueur. Heat just to a boil.

Remove from heat and add chocolate. Stir until chocolate has melted and mixture is smooth. Add eggs, one at a time, beating well after each addition. Gradually blend in flour mixture, then stir in nuts.

Spread batter into a greased and floured 8-inch square baking pan.

Bake for about 30 minutes, until toothpick tests clean.
Let cool completely and cut into 2-inch squares.

Yield: 16 brownies

Brown sugar and the more common white granulated sugar are both obtained from the sugarcane plant.

The plant is stripped of its leaves and then crushed, shredded, and rolled under great pressure to obtain cane juice, which is clarified and boiled. The resulting thick syrup is repeatedly spun in a centrifuge to obtain sugar crystals. These crystals are called raw cane sugar. The raw cane sugar is washed and then dissolved into a water syrup that is filtered to remove impurities. The syrup is boiled, washed, and spun again to obtain crystals. The crystals are the common white granulated sugar.

After there are no more white sugar crystals that can be removed from the syrup, the syrup is processed again, yielding very fine crystals covered with a film of molasses-flavored dark syrup. These fine crystals, technically called soft sugar, are known as brown sugar.

CREAM CHEESE SWIRL BROWNIES

★★★★★★★★★★★★★★★★★★★★★★★★★★★★

SHIRLEY KESSINGER, WEST MEMPHIS, ARKANSAS

> 4 ounces dark sweet chocolate
> 5 tablespoons butter
> 3 ounces cream cheese
> 1 cup sugar
> 3 eggs
> ½ cup plus 1 tablespoon unsifted flour
> 1½ teaspoons vanilla
> ½ teaspoon baking powder
> ¼ teaspoon salt
> ½ cup coarsely chopped pecans
> ¼ teaspoon almond extract

Preheat oven to 350°F.

Put chocolate and 3 tablespoons of the butter in a saucepan or double boiler and heat over simmering water, stirring constantly, until melted. Remove from heat and set aside to cool.

Cream remaining 2 tablespoons of butter with cream cheese until mixed. Gradually add ¼ cup sugar, creaming until light and fluffy. Stir in 1 egg, 1 tablespoon flour, and ½ teaspoon vanilla until blended. Set aside.

In a separate bowl, beat remaining eggs until fluffy. Gradually add remaining ¾ cup of sugar, beating until thickened. Fold in baking powder, salt, and remaining ½ cup flour. Blend in cooled chocolate mixture. Stir in nuts, almond extract, and remaining 1 teaspoon vanilla.

Measure 1 cup of the chocolate batter and set aside.

Spread remaining chocolate batter in a greased and floured 8-inch square pan. Pour cream cheese mixture over top and spread evenly. Drop the set-aside cup of chocolate batter by tablespoons onto the cream cheese mixture. Swirl mixtures together with a knife to marbleize.

Bake for 35 to 40 minutes. Remove and let cool.

Cut into 2-inch squares.

Cover and store in refrigerator.

Yield: 16 brownies

Dr. Brown's sodas—especially the cream and Cel-Ray flavors—have been delicatessen favorites since 1869. (Cel-Ray is the trademarked name for Dr. Brown's celery soda combined with other natural flavors.)

The sodas are kosher, too.

MARZIPAN BROWNIES

★★★★★★★★★★★★★★★★★★★★★★★★★★★

JULIA RICHARDSON, DENVER, COLORADO

3 ounces unsweetened chocolate
½ cup butter
¾ cup flour
¼ teaspoon baking powder
Dash salt
1 cup sugar
2 eggs
1 teaspoon almond extract
7 ounces marzipan

Preheat oven to 350°F.

Place chocolate and butter in a saucepan and heat over hot water until melted. Remove from heat, stir, and then set aside to cool slightly.

Mix together flour, baking powder, and salt. Set aside.

Stir sugar into chocolate mixture and add eggs, one at a time, stirring after each addition. Add almond extract. Blend in flour mixture.

Evenly spread half of the batter into a greased 8-inch square pan. Set aside.

Soften marzipan and roll out into an 8-inch square. Carefully place marzipan on top of batter in pan. Gently spread remaining batter evenly over marzipan layer.

Bake for 20 to 25 minutes.

Remove from oven, let cool completely, and cut into 2-inch squares.

Yield: 16 brownies

BROWNIAN MOTION—*The random, zig-zag motion of microscopic particles suspended in a liquid or gas, caused by collisions between the particles and molecules of the liquid or gas. Brownian motion is named for the Scottish botanist Robert Brown, who discovered it in 1827 while examining plant pollen in water under a microscope. Brownian motion has nothing to do with how quickly brownies move off the plate when you serve them to family or friends.*

POWER BROWNIES

★★★★★★★★★★★★★★★★★★★★★★★★★

DAWN HOBSON, LINCOLN, NEBRASKA

½ cup vegetable oil
½ cup applesauce
½ cup raisins or chopped dates
4 eggs
2 carrots, minced
¾ cup sugar
½ cup cocoa powder
1 cup flour
¼ teaspoon baking soda
Dash salt
¼ teaspoon cinnamon
½ cup unsalted nuts, chopped

Preheat oven to 350°F.

Mix together oil, applesauce, raisins, eggs, and carrots. Gradually add sugar, cocoa, flour, baking soda, salt, and cinnamon. Mix in nuts.

Divide batter into two portions and bake in two greased 8-inch square pans for 20 to 25 minutes, or until toothpick tests clean.

Remove from oven and let cool. Cut into 2-inch squares.

Yield: 32 brownies

FUDGIE-WUDGIES

★★★★★★★★★★★★★★★★★★★★★★★★★

L. JEAN BIEK, NILES, MICHIGAN

½ cup margarine
3 ounces unsweetened chocolate
2 cups sugar
3 eggs
1 teaspoon vanilla
1½ cups flour
Dash salt
1 cup chopped nuts

Preheat oven to 350°F.

Place the margarine and chocolate in a saucepan or double boiler and heat over simmering water until melted. Remove from heat.

Beat in sugar and then add the eggs, one at a time, beating well after each addition. Mix in vanilla, flour, salt, and nuts.

Put batter in an ungreased 8-inch square pan and bake for 30 to 35 minutes.

Cool slightly and cut into 2-inch squares.

Yield: 16 brownies

APRICOT-ALMOND KEEPSAKE BROWNIES

★★★★★★★★★★★★★★★★★★★★★★★★★★★★

BETTE JEAN MINSHULL, EVERETT, WASHINGTON

1 cup butter
4 ounces unsweetened chocolate
2 cups sugar
3 eggs
1 teaspoon almond extract
¾ cup finely cut dried apricots
¾ cup sliced almonds
½ teaspoon salt
1¼ cups sifted flour
1 cup (6 ounces) chocolate chips

Preheat oven to 350°F.

In a large saucepan, melt butter and chocolate over low heat. Remove from heat and stir in sugar. Beat in the eggs, one at a time. Add the almond extract, apricots, and sliced almonds. Fold in salt and flour.

Spread batter in a greased 9 × 13-inch pan and top with the chocolate chips.

Bake for 25 to 30 minutes. Remove from oven and spread softened chocolate chips over brownies while hot.

Let cool and cut into 2 × 3-inch bars.

Yield: 16 brownies

Robert and Elizabeth Barrett Browning were husband-and-wife, nineteenth-century English poets. True romantics, they got married in 1846 after a secret courtship, hiding their love for each other from Elizabeth's tyrannical father.

The couple then left England and lived in Italy until Mrs. Browning died fifteen years later.

MARJORIE'S FUDGY BROWNIES

★★★★★★★★★★★★★★★★★★★★★★★★★★

MARJORIE SMALL, STORM LAKE, IOWA

¾ cup flour
¼ teaspoon salt
½ teaspoon baking soda
½ cup shortening
1 cup packed light brown sugar
1 egg
½ teaspoon butter flavoring
1½ teaspoons vanilla
2 cups quick-cooking oats
1 can (14 ounces) sweetened condensed
  milk
1 tablespoon butter or margarine
6 ounces chocolate
¼ teaspoon black walnut extract
½ cup chopped walnuts

Preheat oven to 350°F.
Sift together flour, salt, and baking soda. Set aside.
Mix shortening, sugar, egg, butter flavoring, and ½ teaspoon of the vanilla. Add flour mixture and oats.

60

Reserve half of mixture. Using dampened hands, press remainder of mixture into a greased 8-inch square pan. Set aside.

Heat sweetened condensed milk, butter, and chocolate over low heat until dissolved. Remove from heat and stir in remaining teaspoon vanilla, walnut extract, and walnuts. Spread over oat mixture in pan.

Using dampened hands, dab reserved mixture over chocolate layer in pan.

Bake for 20 to 25 minutes. Remove from oven and let cool. Cut into 2-inch squares.

Yield: 16 brownies

James Nathaniel Brown—better known as Jim Brown—is one of the greatest running backs in football if not the greatest. He was an all-American fullback—as well as an all-American in lacrosse—at Syracuse University, and the leading rusher in the National Football League for eight out of the nine years he played for the Cleveland Browns. Jim Brown never missed a game due to injury.

CHEWY HONEY FROSTIES

★★★★★★★★★★★★★★★★★★★★★★★★★★★★

PATRICIA MACNAIR, MIDWEST CITY, OKLAHOMA

½ cup butter
½ cup sugar
⅓ cup honey
2 teaspoons vanilla
2 eggs
½ cup flour
⅓ cup cocoa powder
½ teaspoon salt
⅔ cup chopped pecans
Honey Frosting (recipe follows)

Preheat oven to 350°F.

Cream butter and sugar. Blend in honey and vanilla. Add eggs, beating well. Set aside.

Combine flour, cocoa powder, and salt. Gradually add to butter mixture. Fold in nuts.

Pour batter into a greased 9-inch square pan and bake for 20 to 25 minutes.

Remove from oven, let cool, and spread Honey Frosting evenly over top. Cut into 2-inch squares.   Yield: 16 brownies

HONEY FROSTING

3 tablespoons butter, softened
3 tablespoons cocoa powder
¾ teaspoon vanilla
1 cup confectioners' sugar
1 tablespoon milk
1 tablespoon honey

Cream butter and cocoa powder in a small bowl. Add vanilla and sugar. Blend in milk and honey and beat until frosting can be spread easily.

HELEN GURLEY BROWN—*Editor-in-chief of* Cosmopolitan, *who transformed it from a staid magazine for ladies into a lively working woman's guide to sex, career, adventure, and keeping your man and yourself happy with brownies. She also is the author of* Sex and the Single Girl *and* Yesterday's Child, *a book about her mentally disabled daughter.*

DOUBLE-DOUBLE BROWNIES

★★★★★★★★★★★★★★★★★★★★★★★★★★

MATTHEW G. RICE, SARNIA, ONTARIO, CANADA

CHOCOLATE LAYER

2 eggs
¾ cup all-purpose flour
1 cup sugar
½ cup chopped walnuts
Dash salt
¼ cup cocoa powder
½ cup butter or margarine

Beat eggs until foamy. Stir in flour, sugar, walnuts, and salt. Set aside.

Place cocoa powder and butter in a saucepan and cook over low heat until butter melts. Stir mixture well. Remove from heat and add to egg mixture and blend well.

Spread batter evenly in a greased 9 × 13-inch pan. Set aside.

BUTTERSCOTCH LAYER

½ cup butter or margarine
1½ cups brown sugar
2 eggs, beaten
2 tablespoons vanilla
1½ cups all-purpose flour
¼ teaspoon salt
½ cup chopped walnuts

Preheat oven to 350°F.

Cream butter with sugar. Add eggs and vanilla, beating until well mixed. Mix in flour, salt, and walnuts. Spoon over Chocolate Layer in small mounds, spreading as evenly as possible.

Bake for 25 to 30 minutes until brownies begin to pull away from side of pan. Remove from oven and let cool.

BROWN SUGAR
FROSTING

¼ cup butter or margarine
½ cup brown sugar
3 tablespoons milk
1½ cups confectioners' sugar

Bring butter, brown sugar, and milk to a boil in a saucepan. Simmer for 2 minutes. Remove from heat and let cool. Stir in confectioners' sugar. Add more milk or confectioners' sugar, if necessary, to make icing easy to spread.

Spread over cooled brownies in pan.

CHOCOLATE DRIZZLE

4 ounces semi-sweet chocolate
1 to 2 tablespoons butter

Melt chocolate and butter in a saucepan or double boiler over simmering water. Stir to blend.

Drizzle mixture over Brown Sugar Frosting.

Cut into 1 × 2-inch bars.   *Yield: 54 brownies*

PISTACHIO TREATS

★★★★★★★★★★★★★★★★★★★★★★★★★★

JAN PHILIPS, FAIRLAWN, NEW JERSEY

½ cup margarine, softened
1 cup sugar
2 eggs
1 package instant pistachio pudding
¾ cup flour
¼ teaspoon baking powder
¾ cup chopped walnuts
½ cup flaked coconut

Preheat oven to 325°F.

Cream margarine with sugar. Add eggs, one at a time. Gently mix in pistachio pudding. Add flour and baking powder, then fold in walnuts and coconut.

Using dampened hands, pat batter into a greased 8-inch square pan. Bake for 25 to 30 minutes.

Cut into 2-inch squares.

Yield: 16 brownies

PEANUT-BUTTER-CUP BROWNIES

★★★★★★★★★★★★★★★★★★★★★★★★★★

MARYBETH EVANKO, HUMMELSTOWN, PENNSYLVANIA

4 ounces unsweetened chocolate
½ cup butter, softened
½ cup creamy peanut butter
2 cups lightly packed light brown sugar
4 eggs
2 teaspoons chocolate extract
1 cup flour
2 cups (12 ounces) peanut butter chips
12 miniature peanut butter cup candies,
　　cut into quarters

Preheat oven to 325°F.

Melt chocolate in a saucepan or double boiler over simmering water. Set aside to cool slightly.

Cream butter, peanut butter, and brown sugar. Beat in eggs and chocolate extract. Mix in melted chocolate. Blend in flour and peanut butter chips.

Pour batter into a greased 9 × 13-inch pan. Top evenly with peanut butter cup candy pieces, pressing pieces lightly into the batter.

Bake for 30 to 35 minutes. Remove from oven and let cool completely.

Cut into 1½ × 2-inch bars.

Yield: 36 brownies

> *Beautiful, beautiful brown eyes,*
> *Beautiful, beautiful brown eyes,*
> *Beautiful, beautiful brown eyes,*
> *I'll never love blue eyes again.*
>
> —*Old Folk Song*

JESSIE'S BROWNIES

★★★★★★★★★★★★★★★★★★★★★★★★

JESSIE MAE STOCKS, BIRMINGHAM, ALABAMA

½ cup solid shortening
2 ounces unsweetened chocolate
2 eggs
1 cup sugar
¾ cup flour
½ teaspoon salt
½ teaspoon baking powder
1 teaspoon vanilla
2 tablespoons white corn syrup
1 cup pecans
Cocoa Frosting (recipe follows)

Preheat oven to 350°F.

Place the shortening and chocolate in a saucepan or double boiler and heat over simmering water until melted. Remove from heat. Set aside.

Beat eggs and gradually add sugar. Add chocolate mixture and blend well. Set aside.

Sift together flour, salt, and baking powder and gradually add to batter. Blend well. Add vanilla, corn syrup, and nuts, mixing together well.

Pour batter in a lightly greased and floured 8-inch square pan and bake for 25 to 30 minutes.

Remove from oven at very first signs of pulling away from sides of pan. Let cool for 5 minutes on rack, then remove from pan. When almost cool, cover with Cocoa Frosting.

After frosting sets, cut into 1½-inch squares.

Yield: 25 brownies

COCOA FROSTING

¼ cup margarine, very softened
Dash salt
1 teaspoon vanilla
1¾ to 2¼ cups confectioners' sugar
2 tablespoons cocoa powder
Evaporated milk, as needed

Blend margarine, salt, and vanilla. Add 2 tablespoons of the sugar and the cocoa, blending well. Alternately add the remaining sugar and evaporated milk until frosting develops the desired consistency.

BROWNIE PIZZA

★★★★★★★★★★★★★★★★★★★★★★★★★★

DOROTHY LACEFIELD, CARROLLTON, TEXAS

2 ounces unsweetened chocolate
½ cup unsalted butter, softened
1 cup packed dark brown sugar
2 large eggs
1½ teaspoons vanilla
¾ cup flour
Dash salt
6 ounces semi-sweet chocolate, chopped
  into small pieces
3 ounces milk chocolate, chopped into
  small pieces
½ cup chopped pecans
½ cup small pecan halves
3 ounces white chocolate

Preheat oven to 325°F.

Melt unsweetened chocolate in a saucepan or double boiler over simmering water. Remove from heat and set aside to cool.

In a large bowl beat butter and sugar together until light and fluffy. Beat in the eggs, one at a time, mixing well after each addition. Beat in melted chocolate and vanilla until blended. Stir in flour and salt, just until combined. Fold in half of the semi-sweet chocolate pieces, half of the milk chocolate pieces, and all of the chopped pecans.

Scrape batter onto a lightly greased 12-inch-diameter pizza pan and, using a spatula, evenly smooth the surface.

Sprinkle the remaining semi-sweet chocolate pieces, the remaining milk chocolate pieces, and the pecan halves over top of the batter.

Bake on a rack in the center of the oven for 25 to 30 minutes, until toothpick inserted 2 inches from the center comes out clean.

Remove from oven and cool on a wire rack.

Melt white chocolate in a saucepan or double boiler over hot water and then drizzle over top of brownies in pan.

Cut brownies into wedges.

Yield: 16 brownies

BROWNIES—*Members of the Girl Scouts who are in first, second, and third grades, and who might need some re-education in attitudes and values, since they sell packaged cookies instead of homemade brownies.*

CHOCO-CHERRY BROWNIES

★★★★★★★★★★★★★★★★★★★★★★★★

KIERSTEN ROSE VENEZIA, ST. LOUIS, MISSOURI

8 ounces semi-sweet chocolate
6 tablespoons unsalted butter
¼ cup sifted flour
Dash salt
2 large eggs, at room temperature
¼ cup plus 1½ teaspoons sugar
21 ounces prepared cherry pie filling
1 cup mini-marshmallows

Preheat oven to 325°F.

Melt chocolate and butter in a saucepan or double boiler over simmering water. Set aside to cool.

Sift flour and salt. Set aside.

Whisk eggs and sugar until well blended. Whisk in cooled chocolate mixture. Gently fold in sifted flour and salt.

Spread half of batter in an 8-inch square pan that has been lined with foil, greased, and dusted with flour. Set aside.

Strain cherry pie filling, saving the liquid. Spread about three-quarters of the strained cherries over the batter in the pan and then cover cherries with remaining half of the batter.

Bake for 30 to 35 minutes, until top is dry and cracked.

While brownies are baking, stir ¼ cup of the reserved cherry liquid into marshmallows until thoroughly mixed.

When brownies are done baking, remove from oven and spread cherry marshmallows over hot brownies. Cover with foil for about 15 minutes or until marshmallows have melted. Remove foil and let brownies cool completely. Garnish with remaining quarter of the cherries.

Cut brownies into 2-inch squares.

Yield: 16 brownies

The first edition of the Boston Cooking School Cookbook, *popularly known as the* Fannie Farmer Cookbook, *included a recipe for brownies, but they did not contain any chocolate. This grievous shortsightedness was corrected in future editions.*

OLD VIENNA BROWNIES

★★★★★★★★★★★★★★★★★★★★★★★★★★★★

MRS. LOUISE ROSS, ELK GROVE, CALIFORNIA

4 ounces unsweetened chocolate
½ cup butter
½ cup prepared sweetened almond filling
1⅔ cups brown sugar
2 large eggs
1 teaspoon almond extract
¼ cup ground almonds
½ cup flour
Irish Creme Frosting (recipe follows)

Preheat oven to 350°F.

Melt chocolate and butter in a saucepan or double boiler over simmering water. Stir to blend thoroughly.

Remove from heat and stir in almond filling until well mixed. Set aside to cool.

Beat sugar and eggs in a large bowl with electric mixer for 4 minutes. Beat in cooled chocolate mixture, almond extract, ground almonds, and flour.

Spoon batter into a greased and floured 8-inch square pan, spreading evenly.

Bake for 30 to 35 minutes. Remove from oven and cool in pan set on a wire rack.

Cut into 2-inch squares and drop a dab of Irish Creme Frosting on each square.

Yield: 16 brownies

IRISH CREME FROSTING

¾ *cup heavy cream*
1½ *tablespoons confectioners' sugar*
1½ *teaspoons Irish whiskey*
¼ *teaspoon instant coffee powder*

In a chilled bowl and using chilled mixer blades, beat cream with sugar, whiskey, and coffee powder until stiff peaks form.

TOD BROWNING—*American film director (1882–1962) who is considered the creator of the classic horror film. His films include* The Unholy Three *(1925) with Lon Chaney,* Dracula *(1931) with Bela Lugosi, and the critically acclaimed* Freaks *(1932).*

SNOW DROP BROOKIES

★★★★★★★★★★★★★★★★★★★★★★★★★

NORMA TAYLOR, ALBUQUERQUE, NEW MEXICO

> 3 ounces unsweetened chocolate
> ½ cup margarine, softened
> 1 cup sugar
> 2 large eggs
> 2 teaspoons raspberry liqueur
> 1 cup flour
> 1½ teaspoons baking powder
> ¼ teaspoon salt
> 1 cup (6 ounces) white-chocolate chips
> 1 cup chopped nuts

Preheat oven to 350°F.

Melt chocolate in a saucepan or double boiler over simmering water. Remove from heat and set aside.

Cream together margarine and sugar. Beat in eggs, one at a time. Add raspberry liqueur. Set aside.

Sift flour, baking powder, and salt and gradually add to sugar mixture. Stir in chocolate. Add white-chocolate chips and nuts, mixing in well.

78

Drop batter by rounded teaspoonfuls onto a greased cookie sheet. Bake for 8 to 10 minutes, until cookie looks firm and is shiny on top.

Yield: approximately 4 dozen cookies

The Brown Derby Restaurant in Hollywood was the favorite gathering place for the stars and the movers-and-shakers of the motion picture industry. It was the right place to take meetings; do lunch; finagle megadeals; outmaneuver rivals; and create, exchange, and proliferate gossip—all while having brownies for dessert.

RICOTTA-FILLED SQUARES

★★★★★★★★★★★★★★★★★★★★★★★★★★★★

SILVIA MAYNARD, FORT WORTH, TEXAS

½ cup butter or margarine
⅓ cup cocoa powder
2 large eggs
1 cup sugar
1 teaspoon vanilla
½ cup flour
½ teaspoon baking powder
¼ teaspoon salt
Ricotta Filling (recipe follows)

Preheat oven to 350°F.

Melt butter in a saucepan over low heat. Remove from heat and stir in cocoa powder. Set aside to cool slightly.

In a large mixing bowl beat eggs, sugar, and vanilla until light and fluffy. Set aside.

Combine flour, baking powder, and salt, then add to egg mixture, beating in well. Thoroughly blend in cocoa mixture.

Pour half of batter into a greased 8-inch square pan. Smooth to edges (layer will be quite thin). Pour Ricotta Filling over chocolate layer. Spread to edges of pan.

Drop remaining batter by spoonfuls over Ricotta Filling. Use back of spoon to spread top layer of batter gently and evenly over filling.

Bake for 35 to 40 minutes, or until toothpick tests clean. Remove from oven, let cool, and cut into 2-inch squares.

Yield: 16 brownies

RICOTTA FILLING

¾ cup ricotta cheese
2 tablespoons butter or margarine, softened
¼ cup sugar
1 large egg
1 tablespoon flour
½ teaspoon vanilla

Combine all ingredients in a large mixing bowl and beat until creamy.

BROWN BAGGING—*The practice of taking one's lunch to work, usually in a brown paper bag; best if the lunch includes a brownie or two for dessert.*

PEPPERMINT CANDY BROWNIES

★★★★★★★★★★★★★★★★★★★★★★★★★★

FLO BURTNETT, GAGE, OKLAHOMA

2 ounces unsweetened chocolate
⅓ cup vegetable shortening
2 eggs
1 cup sugar
¾ cup pre-sifted flour
½ teaspoon baking powder
½ teaspoon salt
½ cup crushed peppermint candy
½ cup chopped nuts

Preheat oven to 350°F.

Melt chocolate and shortening in saucepan or double boiler over simmering water. Set aside.

In a large mixing bowl, beat eggs, then add sugar. Pour in melted chocolate and shortening, mixing well. Set aside.

Sift flour, baking powder, and salt and gradually add to chocolate mixture. Mix together well. Fold in crushed candy and chopped nuts.

Using dampened hands, spread batter in a well-greased and floured 8-inch square pan. Batter will be thick.

Bake for 30 to 35 minutes, until top has a dull crust. Let cool completely and then cut into 2-inch squares.

Yield: 16 brownies

BLAIR BROWN—*The radiant actress who played the somewhat confused New York City divorcee who was forever trying to get her life together in the television series "The Days and Nights of Molly Dodd." Perhaps her task would have been easier had she eaten more brownies.*

GRASSHOPPER BROWNIES

★★★★★★★★★★★★★★★★★★★★★★★★★

MARILYN A. BARKLEY, GREENUP, ILLINOIS

1 cup sugar
½ cup margarine, softened
4 eggs, beaten
1 cup flour
½ teaspoon salt
1 teaspoon vanilla
16 ounces chocolate syrup
½ cup chopped nuts
Creme de Menthe Frosting (recipe follows)
Chocolate Icing (recipe follows)

Preheat oven to 350°F.

Cream sugar, margarine, eggs, flour, salt, vanilla, and chocolate syrup. Stir in nuts.

Pour batter in a greased 9 × 13-inch pan and bake for 25 to 30 minutes. Remove from oven and let cool.

Spread Creme de Menthe Frosting over brownies and then smooth Chocolate Icing on top of frosting.

Chill in refrigerator, then cut into 2-inch squares.

Yield: 24 brownies

CREME DE MENTHE FROSTING

2 cups confectioners' sugar
½ cup margarine, softened
3 tablespoons creme de menthe liqueur

Mix sugar, margarine, and liqueur together until smooth.

CHOCOLATE ICING

3 ounces chocolate
6 tablespoons margarine

Melt chocolate and margarine in a saucepan or double boiler over simmering water. Stir until smooth.
Remove from heat and let cool slightly.

In the Pennsylvania Dutch Cookbook, published in 1936, the recipe for brownies is called "Neither Cake Nor Candy," a good description of the ethereal nature of brownies.

CINNAMON FUDGE BROWNIES

★★★★★★★★★★★★★★★★★★★★★★★★★★★

JUNE HERKE, HOWARD, SOUTH DAKOTA

4 ounces unsweetened chocolate
½ cup butter
3 eggs
1½ cups sugar
1 teaspoon cinnamon
1 teaspoon vanilla
Dash salt
¾ cup sifted flour
½ cup chopped pecans or walnuts

Preheat oven to 350°F.

Place chocolate and butter in a saucepan or double boiler and heat over simmering water, stirring occasionally, until melted. Remove from heat and set aside.

Beat eggs until foamy. Gradually beat in sugar, beating only enough to ensure that mixture is well blended. Add cinnamon, vanilla, salt, and chocolate mixture, beating until well mixed. Stir in flour and beat just until blended. Stir in nuts.

Pour batter into a greased and floured 8-inch square pan. Bake for

30 to 35 minutes, until toothpick inserted in center comes out almost clean.

Remove from oven and let cool on rack. Cut into 2-inch squares.

Yield: 16 brownies

The members of a nonconformist religious sect, founded in Holland and considered the parent of modern Congregationalism, were called Brownies because they followed the teachings (called Brownism) of the seventeenth-century English clergyman Robert Browne.

RASPBERRY SUPREME

★★★★★★★★★★★★★★★★★★★★★★★★★★★

BERTHA DRISCOLL, BALTIMORE, MARYLAND

BROWNIES ON THE BOTTOM

4 ounces semi-sweet chocolate
1 ounce unsweetened chocolate
6 tablespoons butter
1 cup brown sugar
⅔ cup flour
2 large eggs, beaten
1½ teaspoons instant coffee powder
½ teaspoon chicory
¼ teaspoon red raspberry vinegar
¼ cup seedless raspberry jam

Preheat oven to 350°F.

Place chocolates and butter in a heavy saucepan or double boiler and heat over hot water until melted. Stir well, then set aside.

Mix together sugar, flour, eggs, coffee powder, chicory, and vinegar. Add melted chocolate mixture and stir well.

Pour batter into a greased 8-inch square pan. Bake for 15 to 20 minutes. Do not overbake.

Remove from oven and spread raspberry jam over top of hot brownies. Let cool.

ICING IN THE MIDDLE

5 ounces white chocolate
8 ounces cream cheese
½ cup confectioners' sugar
2 tablespoons raspberry liqueur
½ teaspoon almond extract

Place chocolate in a medium-sized saucepan and heat over hot water until melted. Add cream cheese and mix well.

Remove from heat and add sugar, raspberry liqueur, and almond extract. Mix well.

Spread on cooled brownies.

RASPBERRY GLAZE
ON THE TOP

2 ounces milk chocolate
2 tablespoons butter
3 tablespoons seedless raspberry jam
¼ teaspoon raspberry vinegar

Place chocolate and butter in a medium-sized saucepan and heat over hot water until melted.

Remove from heat and stir in raspberry jam and raspberry vinegar.

Drizzle over Icing in the Middle and cut brownies into 2-inch squares.

Yield: 16 brownies

BROWN PAPER BAG—*Citizen-band radio slang for an unmarked police car . . . and the guy driving it is probably not pulling you over just to offer you some brownies.*

CHEWY TROPICAL BROWNIES

★★★★★★★★★★★★★★★★★★★★★★★★★★★★

THELMA ALLEN JAY, HAVILAND, KANSAS

2 cups sifted flour
½ cup sliced dates
¾ cup butter or margarine, melted
2 cups brown sugar, gently pressed
1 cup sugar
3 eggs
1 teaspoon vanilla
6 tablespoons cocoa powder
½ cup flaked coconut

Preheat oven to 350°F.

Place 2 tablespoons of the flour in a small bowl, add dates, and mix so dates are coated with flour. Set aside.

Put butter, sugars, eggs, and vanilla in a large bowl and mix with an electric mixer on low speed until well blended. Set aside.

Add cocoa powder to remaining flour and sift into sugar mixture, stopping frequently to stir. Fold in coated dates and coconut.

Pour batter into a greased 10 × 15-inch pan.

Bake for 20 to 25 minutes. Remove from oven, let cool, and cut into 2-inch squares.   *Yield: 35 brownies*

MOCHA BOURBONNETTES

★★★★★★★★★★★★★★★★★★★★★★★★★★★

TERRILYNN QUILLEN, INDIANAPOLIS, INDIANA

8 ounces semi-sweet chocolate
¼ cup butter
3 large eggs
½ cup sugar
1 tablespoon brewed coffee and chicory,
   cooled
3 tablespoons bourbon
½ cup unsifted flour
½ cup candied or plain pecans
Butterscotch Mocha Frosting (recipe
   follows)
12 whole candied or plain pecans (as
   garnish)

Preheat oven to 350°F.

Melt chocolate and butter in a saucepan or a double boiler over simmering water. Remove from heat and set aside to cool slightly.

Beat eggs and sugar until lemon-colored. Slowly add coffee and mix very well. Stir in melted chocolate mixture. Add 1 tablespoon of the bourbon and blend well. Fold in flour and the ½ cup of pecans.

Pour batter into a greased and floured 8-inch square pan and bake for 20 to 25 minutes.

Remove from oven and let cool slightly. Poke holes in brownies with a fork or a toothpick and sprinkle the remaining 2 tablespoons of bourbon evenly over surface.

Spread Butterscotch Mocha Frosting on top. Let cool for 1 hour and then cut into 2 × 2½-inch bars. Press a whole pecan into the top of each brownie.

Yield: 12 brownies

BUTTERSCOTCH MOCHA FROSTING

¼ cup (1½ ounces) butterscotch chips
½ cup unsalted butter
1 cup confectioners' sugar
1 teaspoon coffee liqueur
2 teaspoons bourbon

Melt butterscotch chips in a saucepan or double boiler over simmering water. Set aside to cool slightly.

Cream butter and sugar. Stir in melted butterscotch chips, coffee liqueur, and bourbon.

PEANUT-CHOCOCHIPPERS

★★★★★★★★★★★★★★★★★★★★★★★★★★★★

KAREN H. KIM, HONOLULU, HAWAII

½ cup butter or margarine
½ cup vegetable oil
½ cup chunky peanut butter
3 eggs
½ cup sugar
1 cup raw sugar
1 teaspoon vanilla
1½ cups flour
1 teaspoon baking powder
1 cup (6 ounces) semi-sweet chocolate
   chips

Preheat oven to 325°F.

Place butter, oil, and peanut butter in a saucepan. Heat gently until mixture is melted and stir until smooth.

Remove from heat and add eggs, sugars, and vanilla and stir well. Set aside.

Sift flour and baking powder and add to peanut butter mixture. Stir in chocolate chips.

Pour batter into a greased 9×13-inch pan and bake for 20 to 25 minutes.

Cut into 2-inch squares.

Yield: 24 brownies

In the 1930s, an oven was tested to determine if it were working properly by placing a piece of white paper inside and seeing if it turned a nice delicate brown. A "brown-paper oven," as they called an oven that passed this test, was then considered worthy enough for baking brownies.

RICH LEMON FAVORITES

★★★★★★★★★★★★★★★★★★★★★★★★★★

MARJORIE S. TURLEY, PHOENIX, ARIZONA

½ cup butter
4 ounces unsweetened chocolate
1¾ cups sugar
4 eggs
1 cup flour
1 teaspoon vanilla
Lemon Frosting (recipe follows)

Preheat oven to 350°F.

Melt butter and chocolate in a saucepan or double boiler over simmering water. Let cool.

Add sugar and eggs, one at a time, to chocolate mixture, mixing well after each addition. Add flour and vanilla, blending well.

Pour batter into a greased and floured 9 × 13-inch pan and bake for 20 to 25 minutes, until brownies just begin to pull away from sides of pan. Brownies should be moist.

Let cool, cover with Lemon Frosting, and cut into 1½ × 2-inch bars.

Yield: 36 brownies

LEMON FROSTING

¼ cup butter
1 ounce unsweetened chocolate
2 cups or more confectioners' sugar
1 egg
1½ teaspoons vanilla
1½ teaspoons lemon juice
1 cup chopped pecans

Melt butter and chocolate in a saucepan or a double boiler over simmering water. Add 2 cups confectioners' sugar, mixing well. Add egg, vanilla, and lemon juice, blending well. Mix in pecans.

Frosting will harden as it cools. If thicker frosting is desired, add more confectioners' sugar.

Around 1885, Australians started making a cake from flour, fat, sugar, and raisins and calling it a "browny." Not only did they spell it funny, but they used the wrong stuff to make it.

CHOCOLATE MALT BROWNIES

★★★★★★★★★★★★★★★★★★★★★★★★★★

CYNTHIA MARIE MCVAY, MEMPHIS, TENNESSEE

> 1 ounce unsweetened chocolate
> ½ cup butter or margarine
> ¾ cup sugar
> ½ teaspoon vanilla
> 2 eggs
> 1 cup flour
> 1½ teaspoons baking powder
> ½ teaspoon salt
> ½ cup malted milk powder
> ½ cup pecans
> Malted Milk Glaze (recipe follows)

Preheat oven to 350°F.

Melt chocolate in a saucepan or double boiler over simmering water. Remove from heat and set aside.

Cream butter. Add sugar and vanilla. Beat in eggs, then blend in melted chocolate. Set aside.

Sift flour, baking powder, salt, and malted milk powder. Add to chocolate mixture, stirring well. Fold in nuts.

Pour batter into a greased and floured 8-inch square pan. Bake for

25 to 30 minutes. Remove from oven while brownies are still moist. Spread Malted Milk Glaze over brownies. Cut into 2-inch squares.

Yield: 16 brownies

MALTED MILK GLAZE

2 tablespoons butter or margarine, softened
¼ cup malted milk powder
Dash salt
1 cup confectioners' sugar
1 to 2 tablespoons milk

Cream together butter, malted milk powder, salt, sugar, and 1 tablespoon of the milk. Stir in remaining milk, as necessary, to give glaze spreading consistency.

BROWN-EYED SUSAN—*Various plants having bright flowers with dark centers, similar to the black-eyed Susan.*

AMARETTO BROWNIES SUPREME

★★★★★★★★★★★★★★★★★★★★★★★★★★

BETTY J. NICHOLS, EUGENE, OREGON

½ cup butter
2 ounces semi-sweet chocolate
2 eggs, well beaten
¾ cup sugar
½ cup flour
¼ teaspoon salt
½ cup pecans, coarsely chopped
¼ cup amaretto liqueur
Chocolate Amaretto Frosting (recipe
   follows)
White Almond Icing (recipe follows)

Preheat oven to 325°F.

Melt butter and chocolate in a saucepan over low heat. Remove from heat, let cool, then stir in eggs. Add sugar, flour, salt, and pecans, mixing well.

Pour batter in a greased 8-inch square pan and bake for 30 to 35 minutes. Brownies should still be soft. Remove from oven and let cool slightly.

Poke holes in brownies with fork, and pour amaretto liqueur over top.

Refrigerate overnight.

Spread Chocolate Amaretto Frosting over brownies and then drizzle White Almond Icing in a criss-cross pattern on top.

Cut into 2 × 2½-inch bars.

Yield: 12 brownies

CHOCOLATE AMARETTO FROSTING

3 tablespoons butter
1½ cups sifted confectioners' sugar
4½ teaspoons amaretto liqueur
4½ teaspoons cocoa powder
4½ teaspoons hot coffee

Combine butter, sugar, amaretto liqueur, cocoa powder, and coffee and beat until smooth.

WHITE ALMOND ICING

⅓ cup sifted confectioners' sugar
Dash salt
¼ teaspoon almond extract
¼ cup half-and-half

Combine sugar, salt, and almond extract. Add half-and-half, a little at a time, mixing until smooth.

BROWN BETTY—A Pennsylvania-Dutch baked pudding of chopped or sliced apples, bread crumbs, raisins, butter, molasses, sugar, and cinnamon, served with lemon sauce . . . but not nearly as good as brownies.

Buster Brown, along with his sister, Mary Jane, and his dog, Tige, were characters in a very popular newspaper cartoon strip (one of the earliest) created by Richard Fenton Outcault in 1902.

Outcault, seeing the profit potential in licensing his characters, set up a booth at the 1904 St. Louis World's Fair and sold the trademark rights to just about any merchant who passed by. At least fifty products—including harmonicas, soap, soda, coffee, and apples—carried the Buster Brown name.

Buster Brown shoes for children, manufactured and sold by the Brown Shoe Company, is one of only two surviving product lines using the name of Outcault's cartoon character.

The company, named for its founder, George Warren Brown, aggressively promoted Buster Brown shoes in a variety of ways—including stage shows, starring midgets dressed like Buster Brown and accompanied by dogs, that toured the United States and performed in stores and theaters.

The Buster Brown radio show was created in 1943. The show featured Smilin' Ed McConnell as host and included Buster's friends Froggie the Gremlin, Squeeky the Mouse, and Midnight the Cat. In 1951 the program moved to television and was seen until 1954. Andy Devine was the host for the last year of the show, replacing McConnell, who died in 1954.

HAZELNUT KRUNCH QUEEN BROWNIES

★★★★★★★★★★★★★★★★★★★★★★★★★★★

GLEE BRECHLER, MADISON, WISCONSIN

HAZELNUT KRUNCH

1 cup whole hazelnuts, skins removed
1 cup sugar
¼ cup water
3 teaspoons vanilla
1 tablespoon unsalted butter

Preheat oven to 350°F.

Place hazelnuts on a baking sheet and toast for 5 to 8 minutes until nuts are lightly browned. Remove from oven and set aside.

In a heavy saucepan, slowly heat the sugar and water to boiling. Rotate saucepan to swirl ingredients (do not stir). Boil for 2 to 3 minutes.

Remove from heat and add toasted nuts. Stir until nuts are evenly coated with syrup. The sugar will start to crystallize; to melt sugar again and caramelize the nuts, return to medium heat, stirring constantly. If mixture begins to smoke, remove immediately from heat and let cool slightly. Continue to cook and stir mixture until sugar is completely remelted. Stir in vanilla.

Remove from heat and stir in butter.

Spread Hazelnut Krunch mixture on greased aluminum foil and let cool completely. Crumble into coarse pieces. Chop until fine in a food processor fitted with a steel blade. Set aside.

GLEE'S BROWNIES

> 1 cup cocoa powder (preferably Dutch-
> process)
> 1¾ cups sugar
> 1 cup margarine
> 5 eggs
> 1 tablespoon vanilla
> 1½ cups flour

Preheat oven to 350°F.

Sift cocoa powder into sugar and stir until evenly blended. Set aside.

Cream margarine and gradually beat in cocoa mixture. Then beat at high speed for 3 minutes. Add eggs, one at a time, beating and scraping bowl for about 30 seconds after each addition. Beat mixture for 2 more minutes. The batter should be light and fluffy. Stir in vanilla.

Add flour all at once and fold in until blended. Scrape batter into a greased 9 × 13-inch pan and bake for 15 to 20 minutes until brownies are slightly firm to touch. Do not overbake, since brownies should still be moist inside.

Remove from oven and let cool in pan. Set aside.

HAZELNUT KRUNCH FROSTING

1¼ cups confectioners' sugar
½ cup margarine, softened
2 teaspoons milk
1 teaspoon vanilla

Stir sugar, margarine, and milk together. Mix at high speed until light and fluffy. Add vanilla and mix until well blended.

Add 1½ cups of the Hazelnut Krunch and stir together well. Spread over cooled brownies and smooth with a knife.

Cover and chill in refrigerator until cold and firm.

CHOCOLATE FUDGE
GLAZE

8 ounces semi-sweet chocolate
½ cup margarine

Melt chocolate and butter in a saucepan or double boiler over simmering water and stir until smooth.

Pour over frosted brownies, quickly tilting pan so glaze spreads evenly. (You may have to spread it out using a pastry brush.)

Chill in refrigerator until glaze is hard.

Cut into 3-inch squares, then cut each square diagonally to form 2 triangles.

Yield: 24 brownies

MURPHY BROWN—*Who doesn't love the tough-but-kind-hearted journalist played by actress Candice Bergen on fictional newsmagazine program "FYI"? Murphy is the type of character who would steal brownies from fellow staffers, give them to a stray dog . . . and then deny ever doing anything so nice.*

BROWNIE ALASKA

★★★★★★★★★★★★★★★★★★★★★★★★★★★

MILLY AND BUD ABBOTT, ST. MARYS, GEORGIA

> 4 eggs
> 2 cups sugar
> 1 cup butter
> 3 ounces unsweetened chocolate
> 1 cup flour
> 1 cup pecans
> 1 quart vanilla ice cream, frozen very hard
> Almond Fluff (recipe follows)
> Shaved chocolate for garnish

Preheat oven to 350°F.

Cream eggs and sugar. Set aside.

Melt butter and chocolate in a saucepan or a double boiler over simmering water and then add to egg mixture. Mix in flour and pecans.

Pour batter into a greased 9 × 13-inch pan and bake for 25 to 30 minutes. Remove from oven.

Increase oven temperature to 450°F.

Let uncut brownies cool completely, then remove from pan.

Trim uncut brownies into a 6 × 8-inch slab and place on a piece of 7 × 9-inch brown paper. Place on cookie sheet.

Remove ice cream from container and place on top of brownies. Cover top and sides with Almond Fluff, sealing brownies and ice cream completely.

Bake for 4 to 5 minutes until meringue is a delicate brown.

Remove from oven and transfer Brownie Alaska from cookie sheet to a chilled serving plate. Sprinkle with shaved chocolate.

Cut Brownie Alaska into slices and serve at once.

Yield: 6–8 servings

ALMOND FLUFF

3 egg whites
¼ cup sugar
1 teaspoon almond extract

Beat egg whites with electric mixer until stiff. Continue beating while adding sugar, a little at a time, until meringue looks glossy. Add almond extract.

BOURBON PECAN BROWNIES

★★★★★★★★★★★★★★★★★★★★★★★★★★

SHARLENE GENEST, BEDFORD, NEW HAMPSHIRE

> 7 ounces semi-sweet chocolate
> ½ cup unsalted butter
> 2 large eggs
> ¼ cup sugar
> ¼ cup bourbon, or amount to taste
> 1 teaspoon vanilla
> ¼ cup flour
> ¼ teaspoon baking powder
> Dash salt
> 1 cup chopped pecans, toasted lightly
> White Chocolate Frosting (recipe follows)

Preheat oven to 350°F.

Melt 5 ounces of the semi-sweet chocolate and the butter in a saucepan or double boiler over simmering water, stirring until smooth. Remove from heat and set aside to cool completely.

In a large bowl, beat together eggs and sugar until mixture is thick and pale. Beat in bourbon and vanilla. Set aside.

Sift together flour, baking powder, and salt. Add to egg mixture, combining well. Stir in chocolate mixture and pecans.

Pour batter into the middle of a greased and floured 8-inch square pan. Bake for 30 minutes or until brownies pull away from sides of pan.

Remove from oven and let cool on a rack. Spread White Chocolate Frosting over top.

Remove brownies from pan, cut into 2-inch squares, and place on lightly greased cookie sheet. Melt remaining 2 ounces of semi-sweet chocolate and drizzle on tops and sides of brownies.

Yield: 16 brownies

WHITE CHOCOLATE FROSTING

3 ounces white chocolate
1 tablespoon unsalted butter
1 cup confectioners' sugar, sifted
3 to 4 tablespoons milk

Melt chocolate and butter in a saucepan or double boiler over simmering water, stirring until mixture is smooth.

Remove from heat and let cool completely. Whisk in sugar. Slowly whisk in milk until frosting develops desired spreading consistency.

LISA'S FAVORITE TWO-LAYER BROWNIES

★★★★★★★★★★★★★★★★★★★★★★★★★★★★

SUE D. SZWET, DYER, INDIANA

FIRST LAYER

1 cup oats
½ cup brown sugar
6 tablespoons margarine, melted
½ cup flour
¼ teaspoon baking soda
¼ teaspoon salt

Preheat oven to 350°F.

Mix together oats and sugar. Stir in margarine and set aside. Sift flour, baking soda, and salt and slowly add to oat mixture stirring well.

Pat batter in lightly greased 8-inch square pan. Bake for 10 minutes. Remove First Layer from oven.

———

SECOND LAYER

¼ cup margarine, melted
¾ cup sugar
3 tablespoons cocoa powder
1 egg
⅔ cup flour
¼ teaspoon baking powder
¼ teaspoon salt
¼ cup milk
½ teaspoon vanilla
½ cup chopped nuts

Mix together margarine, sugar, and cocoa powder. Beat in egg. Set aside. Sift flour, baking powder, and salt. Add to cocoa mixture along with milk and vanilla, stirring well. Add nuts.

Using a spatula, and being very careful not to touch sides of hot pan, spread Second Layer evenly over baked First Layer and return to oven.

Bake for 25 minutes more.

Remove from oven and let cool.

CHOCOLATE FROSTING

1 tablespoon margarine, melted
1½ tablespoons cocoa powder
¾ cup confectioners' sugar
1 to 2 tablespoons milk

Mix together margarine and cocoa powder, then slowly stir in sugar and milk. Continue to stir until mixture can be spread easily.

Spread frosting over top of baked brownies. Cut brownies into 2-inch squares.

Yield: 16 brownies

"The Unsinkable Molly Brown" was a hit musical on Broadway and a movie starring Debbie Reynolds in the title role. It told the true story of Margaret Tobin Brown who, through force of personality . . . and her husband's gold mines, grew from a rough backwoods girl into the richest woman in Denver in the late 1800s. She was a passenger on the Titanic and survived to tell about it, earning the nickname "Unsinkable."

William Hill Brown wrote The Power of Sympathy, or, the Triumph of Nature *in 1789. His book is generally regarded as the first American novel.*

Edmund Gerald ("Pat") Brown and Edmund Gerald ("Jerry") Brown, Jr., were father-and-son governors of California. Pat held the office from 1959 to 1967, and Jerry from 1975 to 1983. Despite strong grassroots support, neither Governor Brown signed legislation making brownies the official California State Treat.

Brown University (seventh-oldest American college) in Providence, Rhode Island, was founded by the Baptists in 1764 as Rhode Island College. It is now a private, nondenominational institution and a member of the Ivy League. Its name was changed to Brown University in 1804 in recognition of gifts from Nicholas Brown, an alumnus who endowed a chair in oratory and belles-lettres.

CHOCOLATE HEAVEN

★★★★★★★★★★★★★★★★★★★★★★★★★★★★

MRS. HARRIS E. SNEVE, WORLEY, IDAHO

½ cup margarine, softened
1 cup sugar
4 eggs
1 teaspoon vanilla
1 cup plus 2 tablespoons flour
½ teaspoon salt
16 ounces chocolate syrup
½ cup nuts
Chocolate Heaven Frosting (recipe follows)

Preheat oven to 350°F.

Cream margarine and sugar. Beat in eggs, one at a time. Stir in vanilla. Set aside.

Sift flour and salt and add to margarine mixture alternately with chocolate syrup. Mix well. Add nuts and mix well again.

Spread batter in a greased and floured 9 × 13-inch pan. Bake for 25 to 30 minutes.

Remove from oven and cool. Spread with Chocolate Heaven Frosting. Cut into 2-inch squares.

Yield: 24 brownies

CHOCOLATE HEAVEN
FROSTING

6 tablespoons margarine
6 tablespoons milk
1½ cups sugar
3 ounces chocolate

Place margarine, milk, and sugar in a heavy saucepan, heat to boiling, and boil for 30 seconds more.

Remove from heat and add chocolate. Beat until smooth. Let cool.

Can there be any doubt—good grief!—that Charlie Brown and his sister, Sally, the professional eternal children in the "Peanuts" comic strip, love brownies?

CHIPPER-DATE BROWNIES

★★★★★★★★★★★★★★★★★★★★★★★★★★★

TRISTINE D. TESAURO, MOUNT PLEASANT, PENNSYLVANIA

1½ cups (8 ounces) chopped dates
1 cup boiling water
1 cup shortening
1 cup sugar
2 eggs
1 teaspoon vanilla
1¼ cups flour
¼ cup cocoa powder
½ teaspoon baking soda
½ teaspoon salt
1 cup (6 ounces) chocolate chips
½ cup broken walnuts

Preheat oven to 350°F.

Mix dates and boiling water and whip into a thick mixture. Set aside to cool.

Cream shortening, sugar, eggs, and vanilla until light and fluffy. Stir in dates and water. Set aside.

Sift flour, cocoa powder, baking soda, and salt and add to sugar mixture, blending in well.

Pour batter into a greased and floured 9×13-inch pan. Sprinkle with chocolate chips and nuts.

Bake for 25 to 30 minutes. Let cool and cut into 2-inch squares.

Yield: 24 brownies

BROWN COW ICE CREAM SODA—*A delightful combination of root beer and vanilla ice cream with, maybe, a brownie on the side.*

SENSATIONAL STRAWBERRY BROWNIES

★★★★★★★★★★★★★★★★★★★★★★★★★

SANDRA E. RYGLE, CARMICHAELS, PENNSYLVANIA

6 tablespoons butter
3 ounces unsweetened chocolate
1 cup flour
3 tablespoons cocoa powder
½ teaspoon salt
1½ cups sugar
3 tablespoons confectioners' sugar
2 large eggs, at room temperature
3 tablespoons seedless strawberry jam
½ teaspoon red wine vinegar
½ cup toasted blanched almonds, coarsely
  chopped
Strawberry Jam Topping (recipe follows)
Chocolate Strawberry Glaze (recipe
  follows)
16 small whole strawberries

Preheat oven to 325°F.

Combine butter and chocolate in a heavy saucepan or double boiler and melt over simmering water. Stir until smooth. Remove from heat and set aside to cool.

Sift flour, cocoa powder, and salt and set aside.

Combine sugars and then add eggs, beating with an electric mixer until mixture turns pale yellow. Add strawberry jam and vinegar, continuing to beat for 1 minute more. Fold in cooled chocolate mixture. Fold in flour mixture. Add almonds, mixing together well.

Spread batter evenly in a greased and floured 8-inch square pan. Bake on a rack in the lower third of oven for 30 to 35 minutes, or until wooden toothpick inserted in brownies comes out almost clean.

Remove from oven and spread Strawberry Jam Topping evenly over hot brownies. Let cool completely.

Spread Chocolate Strawberry Glaze over top and let stand for at least 2 hours, until chocolate sets.

Cut into 2-inch squares and garnish each brownie with a fresh strawberry.

Yield: 16 brownies

STRAWBERRY JAM TOPPING

¼ cup seedless strawberry jam
¼ teaspoon red wine vinegar

Combine strawberry jam and vinegar and stir until completely blended.

CHOCOLATE STRAWBERRY GLAZE

2 ounces semi-sweet chocolate
3 tablespoons seedless strawberry jam
2 tablespoons butter
⅛ teaspoon red wine vinegar

In a heavy saucepan combine chocolate, jam, butter, and vinegar and cook over low heat, stirring until mixture is smooth.
Remove from heat and let mixture cool for about 25 minutes.

The pet duck of cartoonist and "Simpsons" creator Matt Groening is named Brownie, and one can assume that Brownie gladly shares his brownies with young Bart.

DOC BROWN—*The frenetic inventor of the time-traveling DeLorean, played by Christopher Lloyd in the "Back to the Future" movie series. Doc Brown traveled forward and backward and backward and forward in time, probably searching for the best brownies ever made.*

Under a system devised by George R. Brown, general superintendent of the Fall Brook Railway (later part of the New York Central system), demerits were given to railroad workers who broke company rules. These demerits, called "brownies," were a more lenient punishment than the outright firing of workers for infractions. Giving "brownies" was also less severe than taking away a worker's lunchtime brownies.

BRAZILIAN RAIN FOREST BROWNIES

★★★★★★★★★★★★★★★★★★★★★★★★★★

ELLEN BURR, TRURO, MASSACHUSETTS

4 ounces unsweetened chocolate
4 ounces unsalted butter
4 eggs
¼ cup coffee liqueur
1 cup mashed ripe red or yellow bananas
2 cups sugar
2 teaspoons vanilla
1 cup flour
1 teaspoon cinnamon
1 cup Brazil nuts, chopped
½ cup cashew halves
3 tablespoons raw sugar

Preheat oven to 350°F.

Melt chocolate and butter in a saucepan or double boiler over simmering water. Set aside.

In a large mixing bowl, beat eggs until frothy. Beat in coffee liqueur, bananas, sugar, and vanilla. Stir in chocolate mixture, blending well. Set aside.

Sift flour and cinnamon and then add to batter. Fold in Brazil nuts. Pour batter into a well-greased 8-inch square pan. Press cashew halves lightly into batter and sprinkle with raw sugar.

Bake for 50 minutes or until center tests clean with a toothpick. Cool on rack, then cut into 2-inch squares.

Yield: 16 brownies

BROWN STUDY—*A state of deep thought or daydreaming—even if thoughts are not about brownies.*

Now that you have the recipes for the 55 best brownies in the world, here are the 92 best places in the United States to eat them:

Browns, Alabama
Brownsboro, Alabama
Brownville, Alabama
Brownstown, Arkansas
Brownsville, Arkansas
Browns Valley, California
Brownsville, California
Browns Farm, Florida
Brownville, Florida
Brownsville, Florida
Brown Dale, Georgia
Brown's Crossing, Georgia
Browntown, Georgia
Brown County, Illinois
Brownfield, Illinois
Browning, Illinois
Browns, Illinois
Brownstown, Illinois
Brownsville, Illinois
Brown County, Indiana
Brownsburg, Indiana

Brownstown, Indiana (both of them)
Browns Valley, Indiana
Brownsville, Indiana
Brown County, Kansas
Brownell, Kansas
Brownsboro, Kentucky
Browns Valley, Kentucky
Brownsville, Kentucky
Brownsville-Bawcomville, Louisiana
Brownfield, Maine
Brownville, Maine
Brownville Junction, Maine
Browning Mill, Maryland
Browns Corner, Maryland
Brownsville, Maryland
Brown City, Michigan
Brownlee Park, Michigan
Brown County, Minnesota
Brownsdale, Minnesota
Browns Valley, Minnesota
Brownsville, Minnesota
Brownton, Minnesota
Brownfield, Mississippi
Brownbranch, Missouri

Browning, Missouri
Brownington, Missouri
Browns Station, Missouri
Brownwood, Missouri
Browning, Montana
Brown County, Nebraska
Brownlee, Nebraska
Brownson, Nebraska
Brownville, Nebraska
Browns, New Jersey
Brown Mills, New Jersey
Browntown, New Jersey
Brownville, New York
Browns Summit, North Carolina
Brown County, Ohio
Brownsville, Ohio
Browning, Oklahoma
Brownsboro, Oregon
Brownsville, Oregon
Brown, Pennsylvania
Brownfield, Pennsylvania
Brownsdale, Pennsylvania
Brownstown, Pennsylvania (both of them)
Brownsville, Pennsylvania

Brownsville, South Carolina
Brown County, South Dakota
Brownsville, Tennessee
Brown County, Texas
Browndell, Texas
Brownfield, Texas
Brownsboro, Texas
Brownsville, Texas
Brownwood, Texas
Brownington Center, Vermont
Brownsville, Vermont
Brownsburg, Virginia
Browntown, Virginia
Brownstown, Washington
Brown's Chapel, West Virginia
Browns Mills, West Virginia
Brown County, Wisconsin
Brown Deer, Wisconsin
Browns Lake, Wisconsin
Brownsville, Wisconsin
Browntown, Wisconsin

INDEX

★★★★★★★★★★★★★★★★★★★★★★★★★

131